HOW TO DRAW SUPER HEROES

Illustrated by Jael

Kidsbooks Incorporated

Copyright © 1993 Kidsbooks Inc.
3535 West Peterson Avenue
Chicago, IL 60659

Manufactured in the United States of America

INTRODUCTION

This book will show you how to draw lots of different superheroes. Some are more difficult than others, but if you follow along, step-by-step, you'll soon be able to draw any superhero you wish.

SUPPLIES

NUMBER 2 PENCILS   FELT-TIP PEN
SOFT ERASER   COLORED PENCILS, MARKERS,
DRAWING PAD   OR CRAYONS

Each figure in this book begins with a **line or stick figure**. This establishes the movement of the superhero. Then, different kinds of **oval** shapes are added over the line figure to round out the basic sections of the body. Other shapes will also be used.

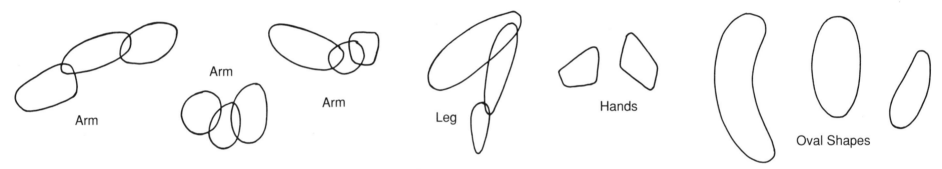

Arm

Arm

Arm

Leg

Hands

Oval Shapes

The basic shapes usually overlap when forming the arms and legs.

The first two steps create a **solid foundation** of the figure — much like a builder who must first construct a foundation before building the rest of the house. Next comes the fun part — creating the muscles, face, clothing, armor and weapons, and adding all the details and finishing touches.

HELPFUL HINTS:

1. Following the first two steps carefully will make the final steps easier.
2. **Always keep your pencil lines light and soft**. These "guide-lines" will be easier to erase when you no longer need them.
3. Don't be afraid to erase. It usually takes lots of drawing and erasing before you will be satisfied with the way your superhero or superheroine looks.

4. Add details and all the finishing touches **after** you have blended and refined all the shapes and your figure is complete.
5. You can check a pose by using yourself as a model. Just stand in front of a full-length mirror.
6. Remember: Practice Makes Perfect. Don't be discouraged if you can't get the "hang of it" right away. Just keep drawing and erasing until you do.

HOW TO START

1. Begin by drawing a stick figure like the one on this page. This will help you make the figure move in the right direction. The action and movement of a figure is called **gesture.**
2. Add the oval shapes to the stick figure. Note that many of these ovals are not "perfect." These are the basic guidelines that form the body and create the foundation.

REMEMBER TO KEEP YOUR LINES LIGHTLY DRAWN

Foreshortening
Superheroes are shown in dramatic poses that include foreshortening. To understand this better, stand in front of a mirror and point to yourself with one arm. See how short your arm appears? Then hold your other arm straight out to your side. Now you can see your arm's normal length. An artist learns to draw things as the eye sees them, not as they really are. This gives the figure a realistic, 3-dimensional appearance.

3. Carefully draw the body muscles **within** the oval guidelines. The dotted lines show what can be erased as you go along. When you are satisfied with your drawing, erase the guidelines, including the stick figure.
4. Add facial features, hair, clothing, and all the other details and finishing touches to complete your superhero drawing.
   Color your finished superheroes with your favorite colors or, for a more dramatic effect, outline them with a thick, black marker.

Elsewhere in this book you will find illustrations of superhero weapons, as well as futuristic spacecraft and cities. These are just **examples** of things you can add to a finished picture. Use your **imagination** and create different objects and backgrounds to enhance your superhero drawings.
   When you have drawn some or all of the superheroes in this book, and are comfortable with the drawing technique, start creating your own superheroes.
   Most of all, **HAVE FUN!**

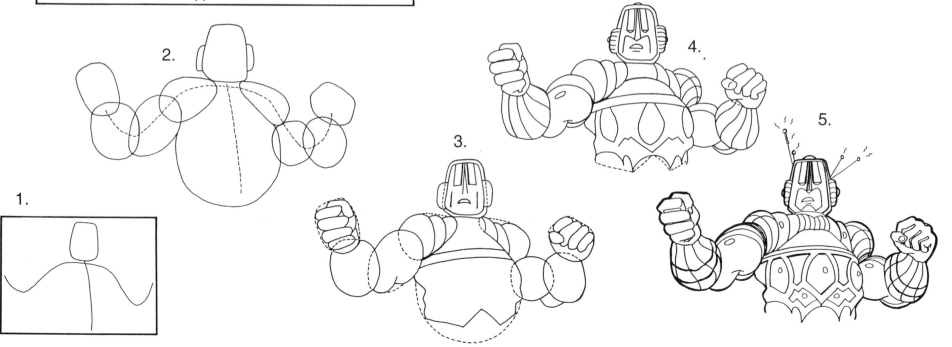

BLADE RIDER

1.

3. Start defining and shaping the muscles within the oval guidelines, erasing your gesture lines as you go along. Then, begin outlining this superhero's hair, hands, and face.

1.& 2. Starting with the head, draw the simple stick figure (gesture lines). Then add the various ovals and other guideline shapes.

2.

Use foreshortening when any part of the body points away from or toward, you, the viewer. This gives your figure a dramatic, 3-dimensional look.

Note: Keep all your guidelines lightly drawn. They will be easier to erase later on.

Before going to the next step, make sure that you are satisfied with the way your drawing looks.

5. Now add all the final details and finishing touches, and Blade Rider is ready for action!

4. Complete the facial features and sharply define Blade Rider's arms, legs, and chest muscles. Then, begin adding clothes and details.

BOLT-MAN

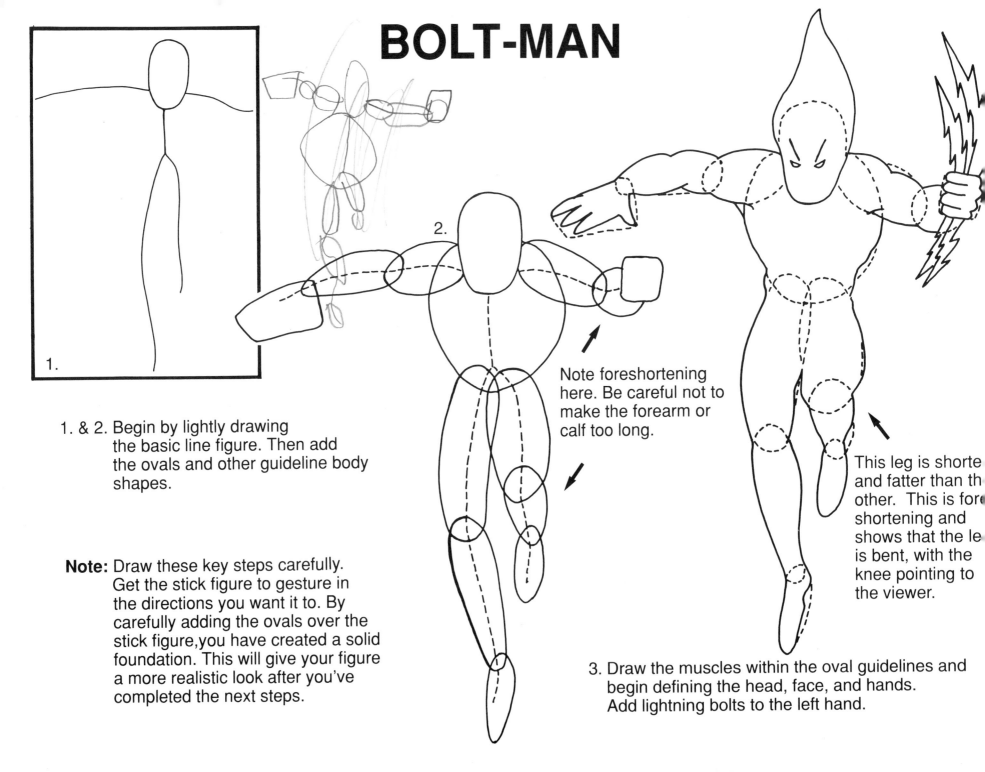

1.

2.

Note foreshortening here. Be careful not to make the forearm or calf too long.

1. & 2. Begin by lightly drawing the basic line figure. Then add the ovals and other guideline body shapes.

Note: Draw these key steps carefully. Get the stick figure to gesture in the directions you want it to. By carefully adding the ovals over the stick figure, you have created a solid foundation. This will give your figure a more realistic look after you've completed the next steps.

This leg is shorte and fatter than th other. This is fore shortening and shows that the le is bent, with the knee pointing to the viewer.

3. Draw the muscles within the oval guidelines and begin defining the head, face, and hands. Add lightning bolts to the left hand.

Erase any unnecessary guidelines.

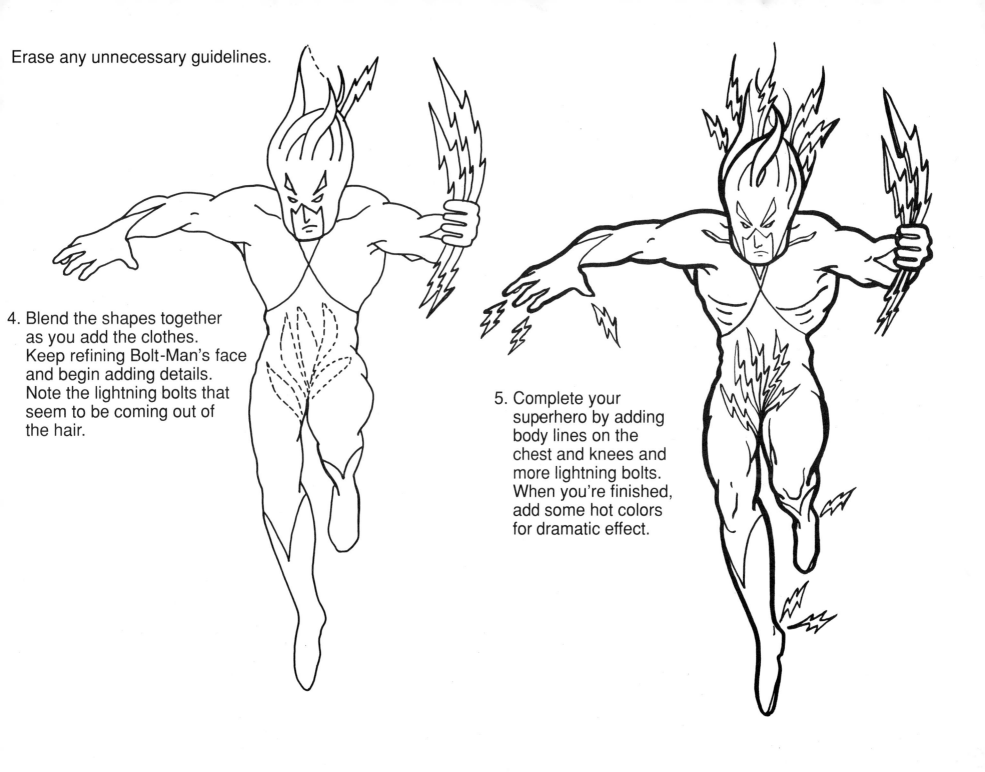

4. Blend the shapes together
   as you add the clothes.
   Keep refining Bolt-Man's face
   and begin adding details.
   Note the lightning bolts that
   seem to be coming out of
   the hair.

5. Complete your
   superhero by adding
   body lines on the
   chest and knees and
   more lightning bolts.
   When you're finished,
   add some hot colors
   for dramatic effect.

LEKTRA

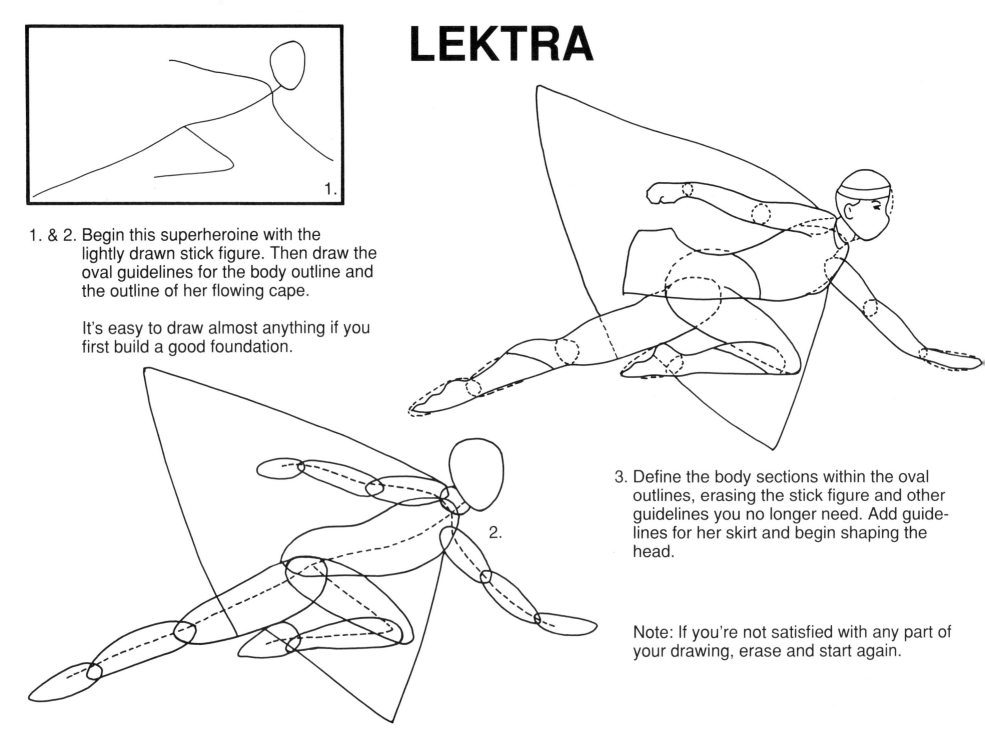

1. & 2. Begin this superheroine with the lightly drawn stick figure. Then draw the oval guidelines for the body outline and the outline of her flowing cape.

It's easy to draw almost anything if you first build a good foundation.

3. Define the body sections within the oval outlines, erasing the stick figure and other guidelines you no longer need. Add guidelines for her skirt and begin shaping the head.

Note: If you're not satisfied with any part of your drawing, erase and start again.

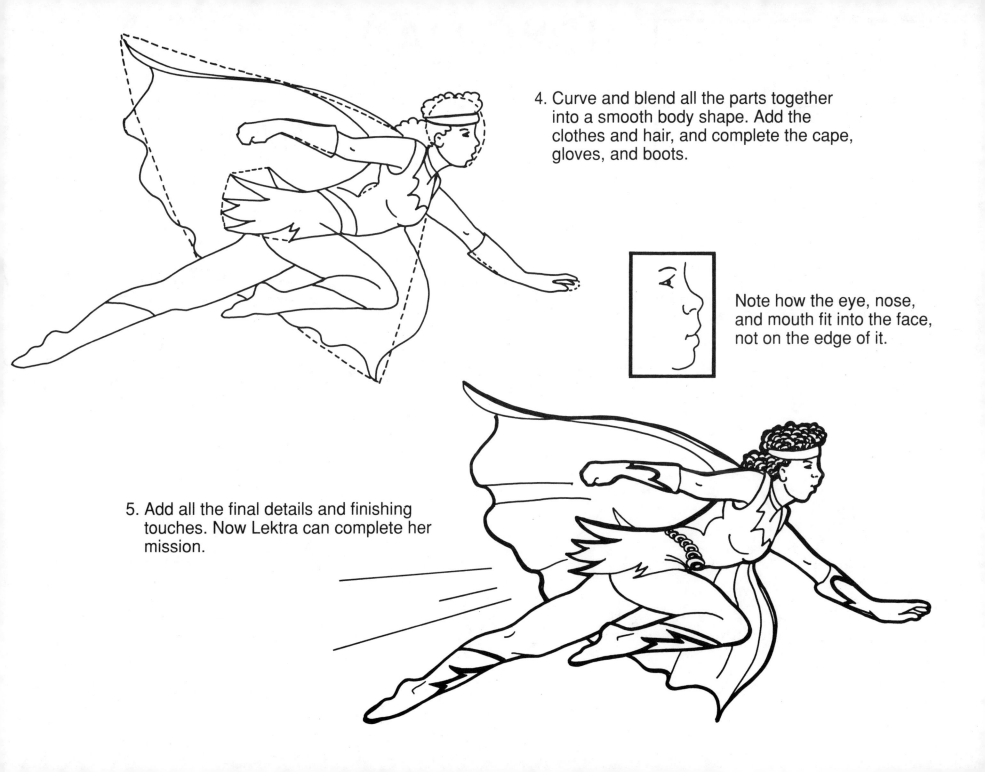

4. Curve and blend all the parts together into a smooth body shape. Add the clothes and hair, and complete the cape, gloves, and boots.

Note how the eye, nose, and mouth fit into the face, not on the edge of it.

5. Add all the final details and finishing touches. Now Lektra can complete her mission.

ROBO-MAN

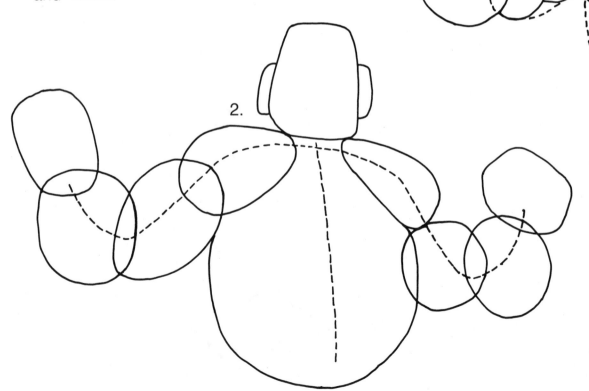

1.

1. & 2. Draw the gesture lines. Then add the guideline shapes for the head, arms, and torso.

2.

3. Draw the simple shapes on Robo-Man's face and carefully add the fingers. Define the torso and arm sections, erasing any unnecessary guidelines as you go along.

Remember to keep all your guidelines lightly drawn, so that they may be easily erased.

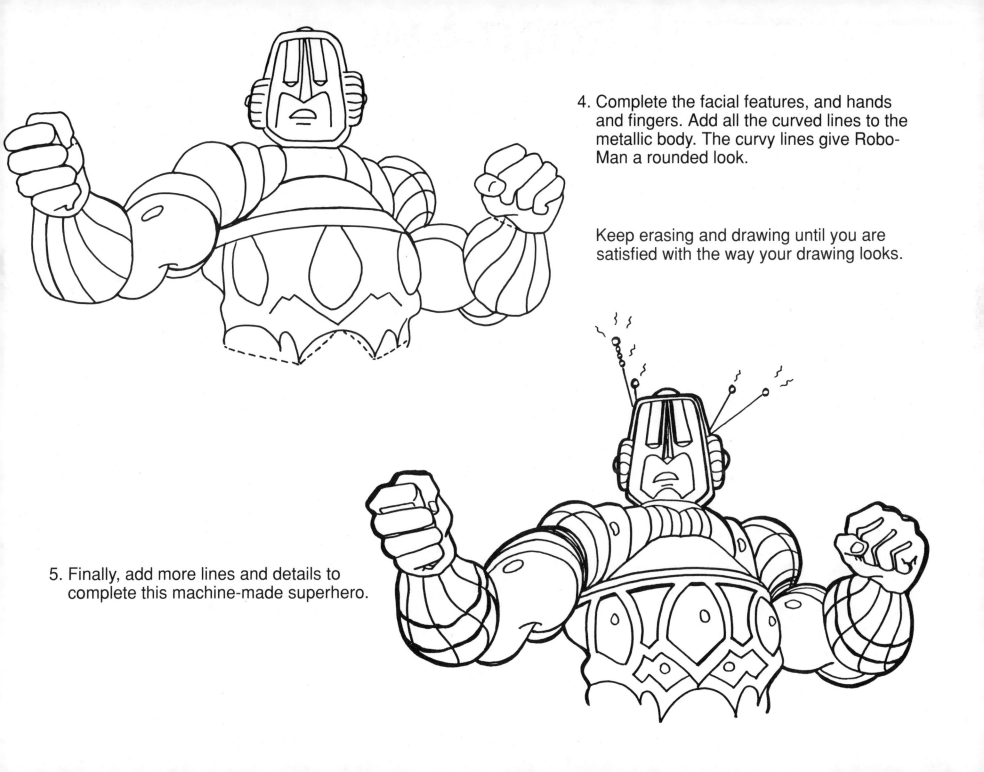

4. Complete the facial features, and hands and fingers. Add all the curved lines to the metallic body. The curvy lines give Robo-Man a rounded look.

Keep erasing and drawing until you are satisfied with the way your drawing looks.

5. Finally, add more lines and details to complete this machine-made superhero.

ZANTRON

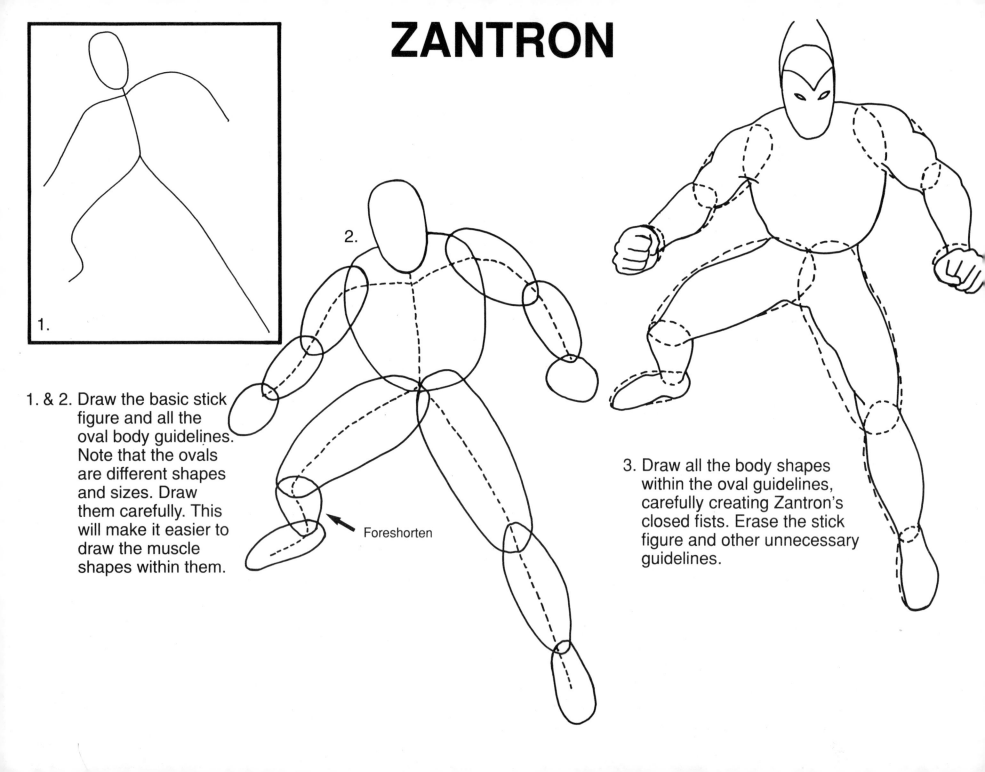

1.

2.

Foreshorten

1. & 2. Draw the basic stick figure and all the oval body guidelines. Note that the ovals are different shapes and sizes. Draw them carefully. This will make it easier to draw the muscle shapes within them.

3. Draw all the body shapes within the oval guidelines, carefully creating Zantron's closed fists. Erase the stick figure and other unnecessary guidelines.

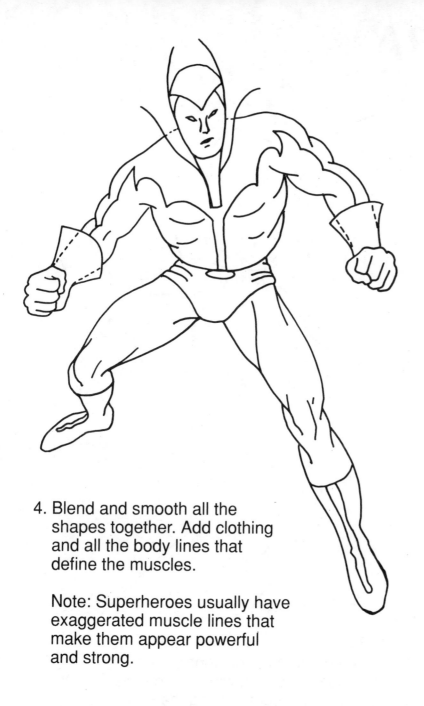

4. Blend and smooth all the shapes together. Add clothing and all the body lines that define the muscles.

Note: Superheroes usually have exaggerated muscle lines that make them appear powerful and strong.

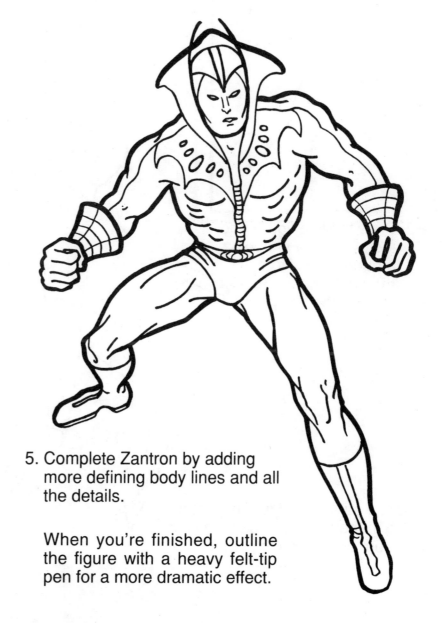

5. Complete Zantron by adding more defining body lines and all the details.

When you're finished, outline the figure with a heavy felt-tip pen for a more dramatic effect.

ZEPHRA

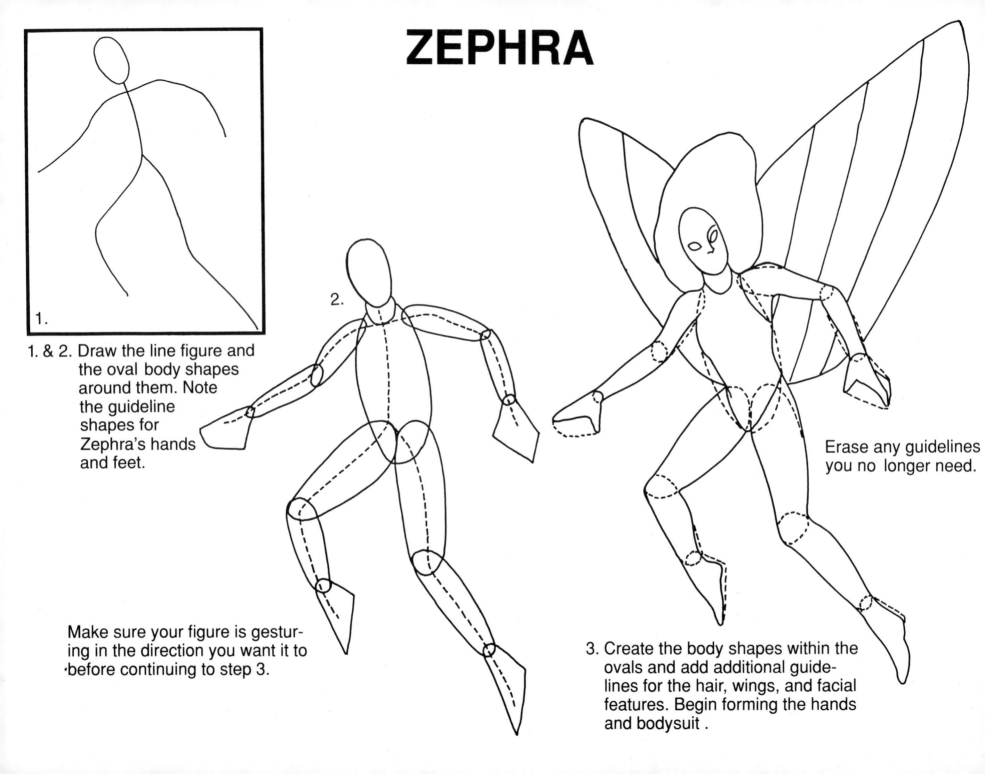

1.

1. & 2. Draw the line figure and the oval body shapes around them. Note the guideline shapes for Zephra's hands and feet.

Make sure your figure is gesturing in the direction you want it to before continuing to step 3.

2.

Erase any guidelines you no longer need.

3. Create the body shapes within the ovals and add additional guidelines for the hair, wings, and facial features. Begin forming the hands and bodysuit.

4. Blend the body parts together; complete the facial features; and finish drawing the hands. Zephra has beautiful, feathered wings. Starting close to her body — from the inside out — draw the feathers. Lastly, draw her flowing, wavy hair and begin adding details to her outfit.

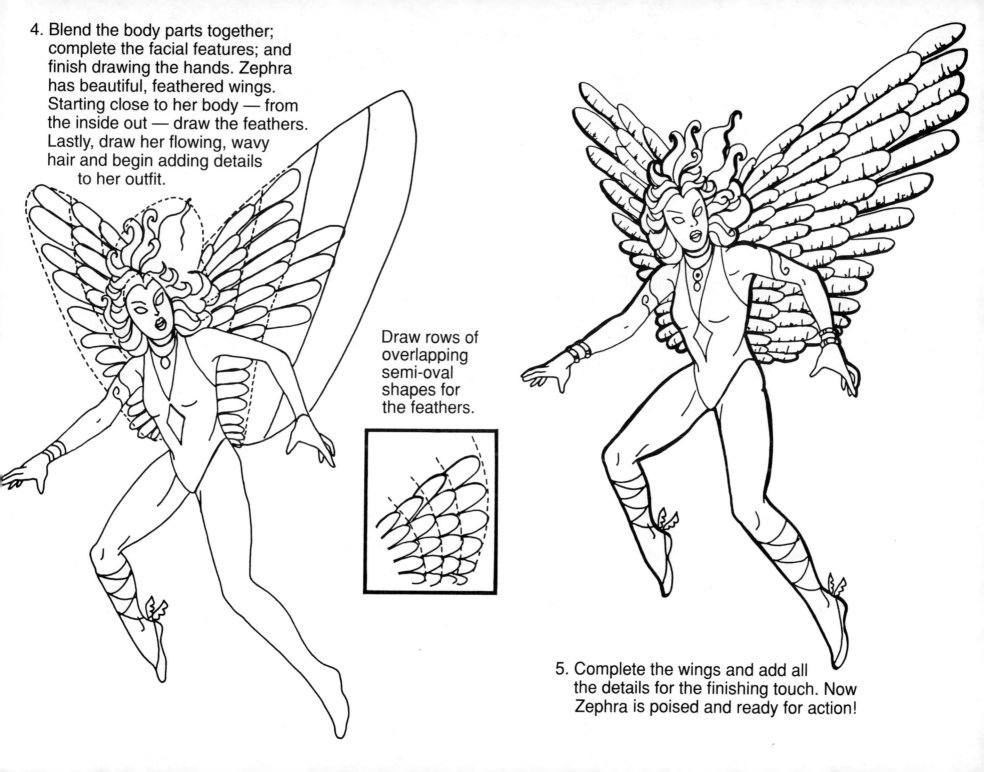

Draw rows of overlapping semi-oval shapes for the feathers.

5. Complete the wings and add all the details for the finishing touch. Now Zephra is poised and ready for action!

Here are a few examples of the kind of city a superhero might
come from. Try drawing these, then use your imagination to create others.
Backgrounds will give your drawing a "finished" look.

Another futuristic city on a distant planet.

QUASAR-MAN

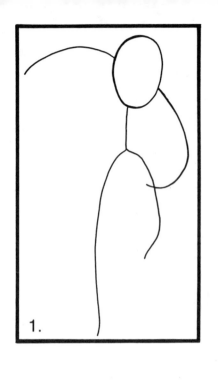

1.

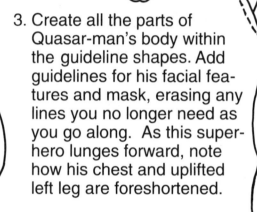

2.

1. & 2. Starting with the oval-shaped head, draw the stick figure. Add the broad body shapes for the super muscles, and the board beneath the right foot.

Remember to keep these guidelines lightly drawn.

3. Create all the parts of Quasar-man's body within the guideline shapes. Add guidelines for his facial features and mask, erasing any lines you no longer need as you go along. As this superhero lunges forward, note how his chest and uplifted left leg are foreshortened.

Note: Step 3 is a very important step. It establishes the basic overall structure and look of your drawing. In steps 4 and 5, you are simply refining and adding details to the figure you have created.

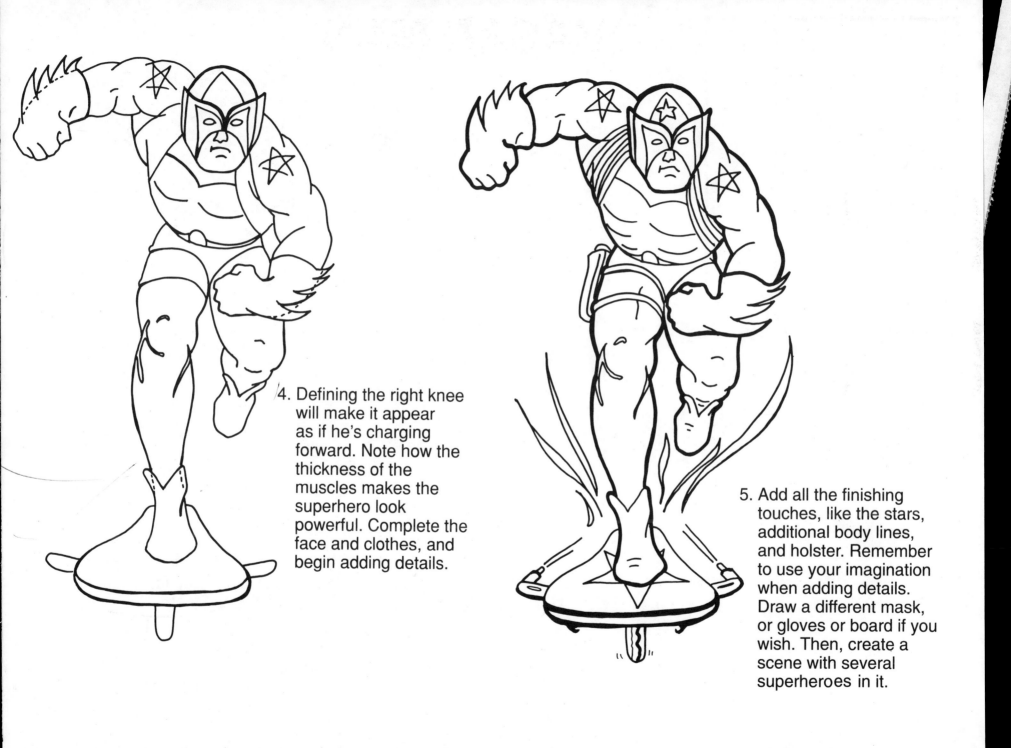

4. Defining the right knee will make it appear as if he's charging forward. Note how the thickness of the muscles makes the superhero look powerful. Complete the face and clothes, and begin adding details.

5. Add all the finishing touches, like the stars, additional body lines, and holster. Remember to use your imagination when adding details. Draw a different mask, or gloves or board if you wish. Then, create a scene with several superheroes in it.

GIGANTO

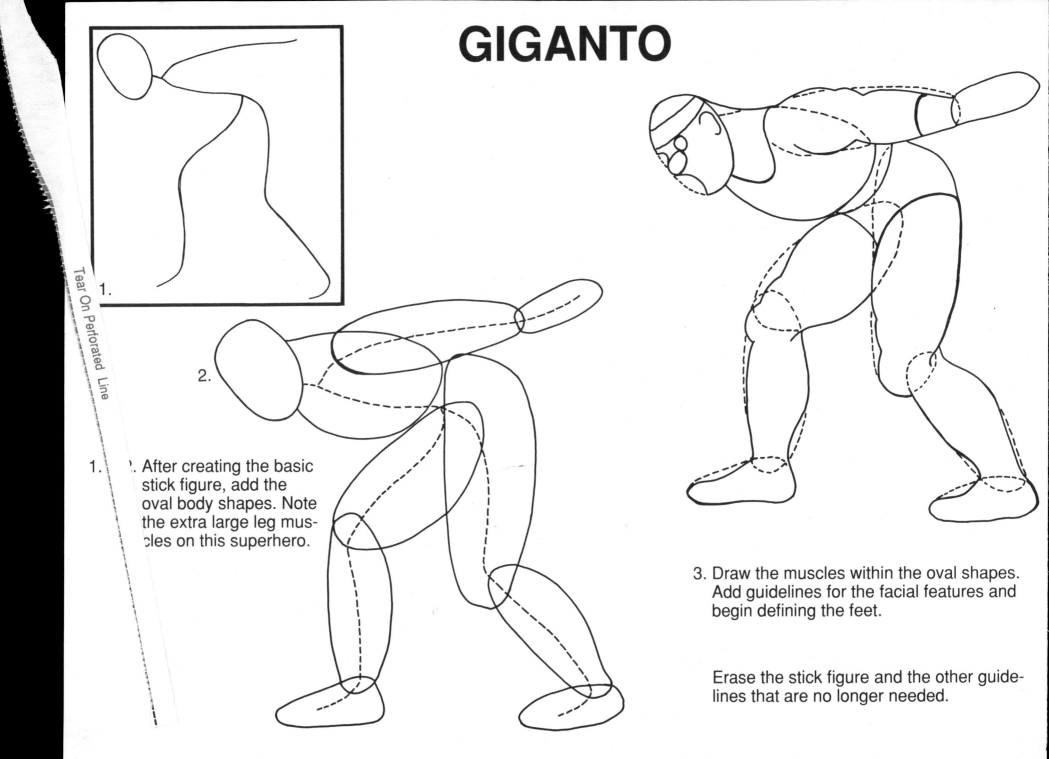

1.

2.

1. After creating the basic stick figure, add the oval body shapes. Note the extra large leg muscles on this superhero.

3. Draw the muscles within the oval shapes. Add guidelines for the facial features and begin defining the feet.

Erase the stick figure and the other guidelines that are no longer needed.

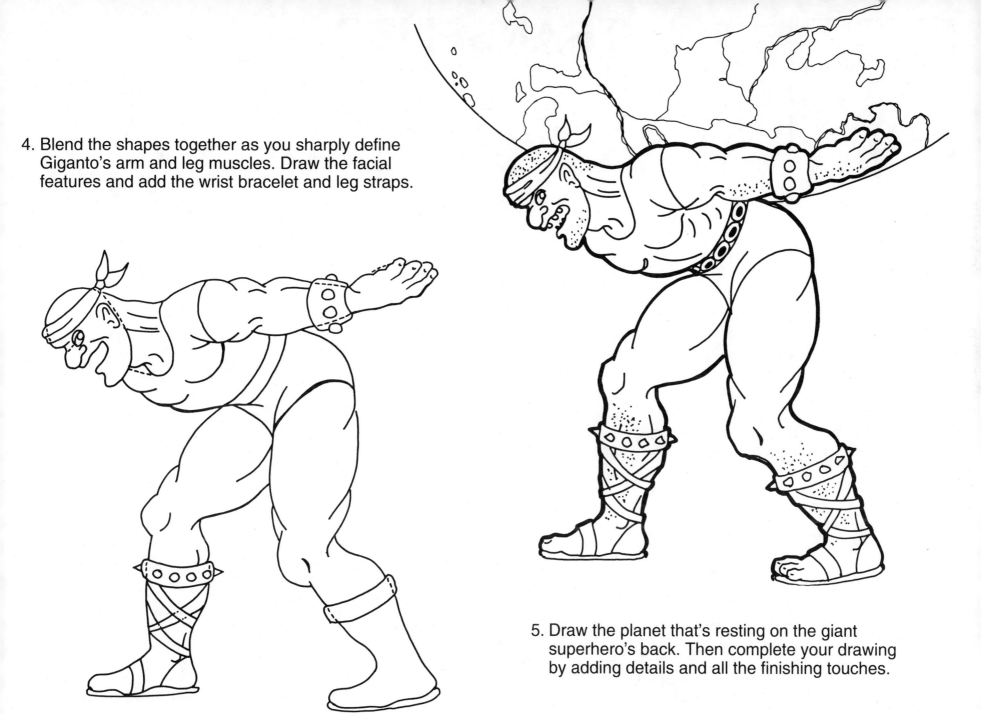

4. Blend the shapes together as you sharply define Giganto's arm and leg muscles. Draw the facial features and add the wrist bracelet and leg straps.

5. Draw the planet that's resting on the giant superhero's back. Then complete your drawing by adding details and all the finishing touches.

TRANSFLIER

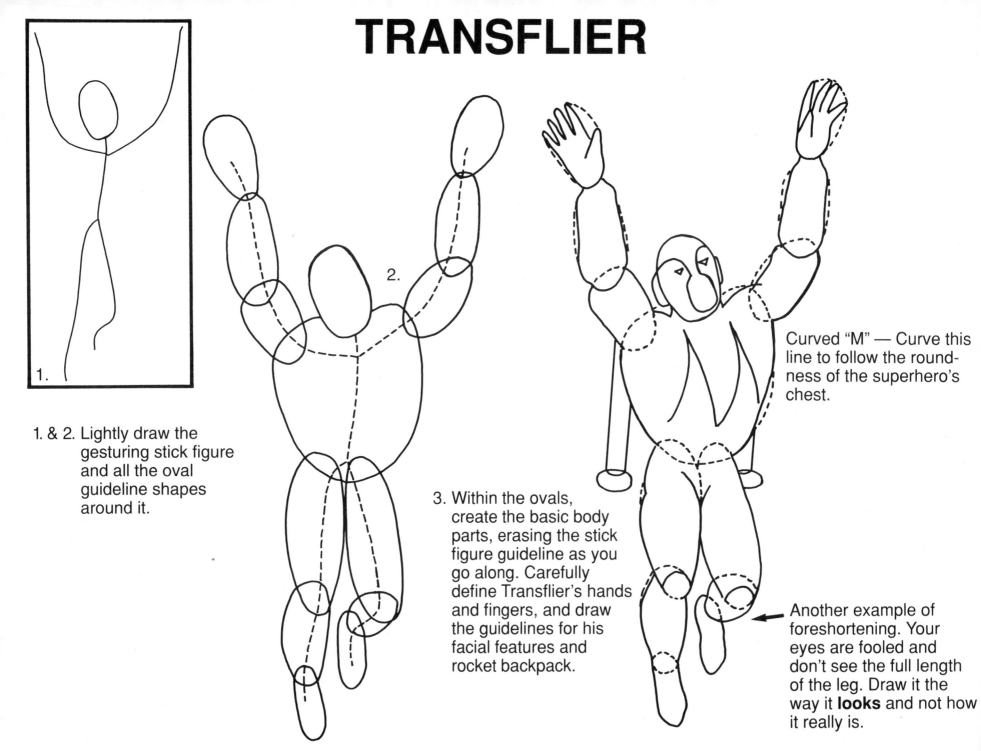

1.

2.

1. & 2. Lightly draw the
gesturing stick figure
and all the oval
guideline shapes
around it.

3. Within the ovals,
create the basic body
parts, erasing the stick
figure guideline as you
go along. Carefully
define Transflier's hands
and fingers, and draw
the guidelines for his
facial features and
rocket backpack.

Curved "M" — Curve this
line to follow the round-
ness of the superhero's
chest.

Another example of
foreshortening. Your
eyes are fooled and
don't see the full length
of the leg. Draw it the
way it **looks** and not how
it really is.

4. Blend and shape all the forms together, paying close attention to the curved lines on the arms and legs. Continue working on the face and fingers, and begin adding details.

5. Add lots more details to complete Transflier. When you're finished, add exhaust lines to the rocket so that he can zoom away.

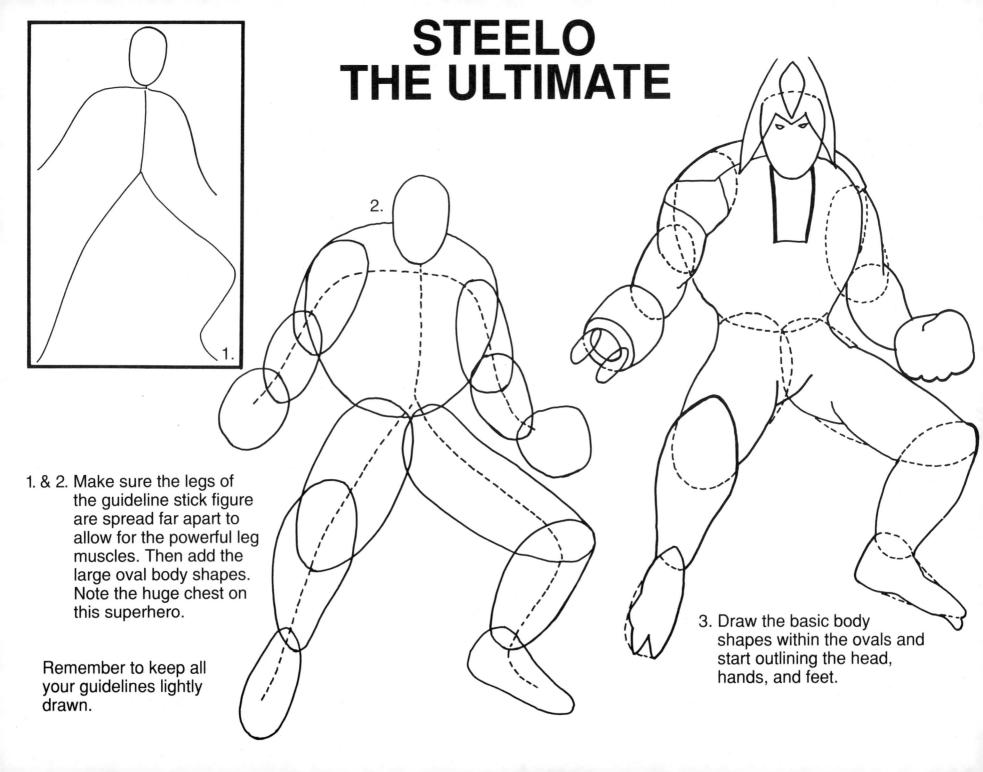

STEELO
THE ULTIMATE

1.

2.

1. & 2. Make sure the legs of the guideline stick figure are spread far apart to allow for the powerful leg muscles. Then add the large oval body shapes. Note the huge chest on this superhero.

Remember to keep all your guidelines lightly drawn.

3. Draw the basic body shapes within the ovals and start outlining the head, hands, and feet.

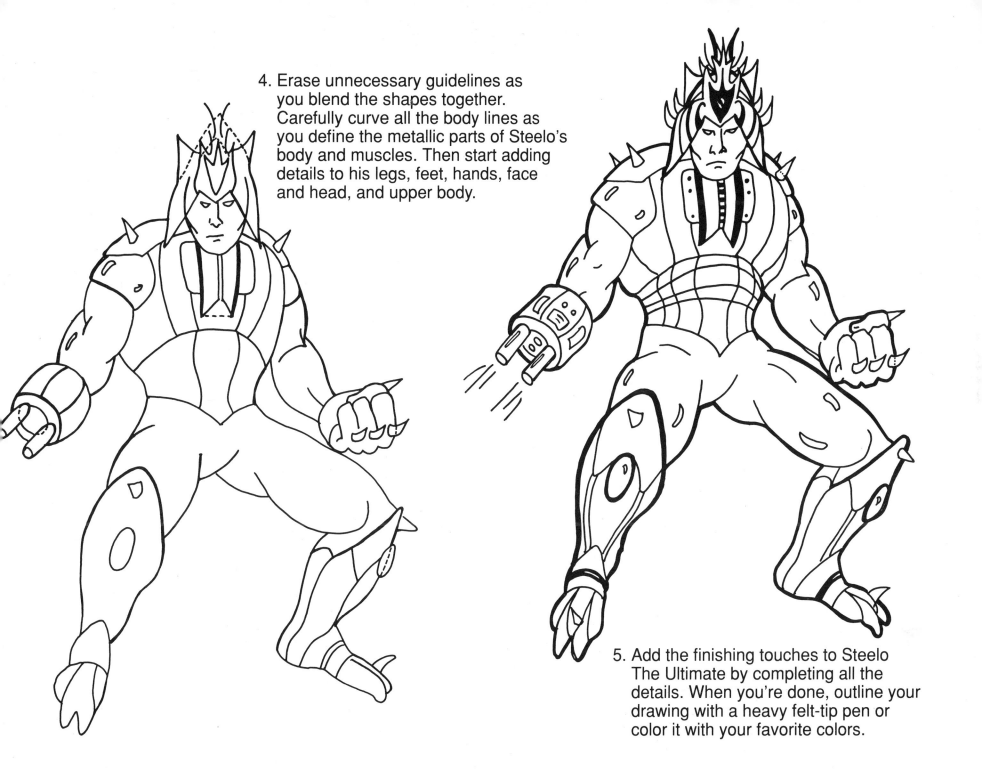

4. Erase unnecessary guidelines as you blend the shapes together. Carefully curve all the body lines as you define the metallic parts of Steelo's body and muscles. Then start adding details to his legs, feet, hands, face and head, and upper body.

5. Add the finishing touches to Steelo The Ultimate by completing all the details. When you're done, outline your drawing with a heavy felt-tip pen or color it with your favorite colors.

THORA

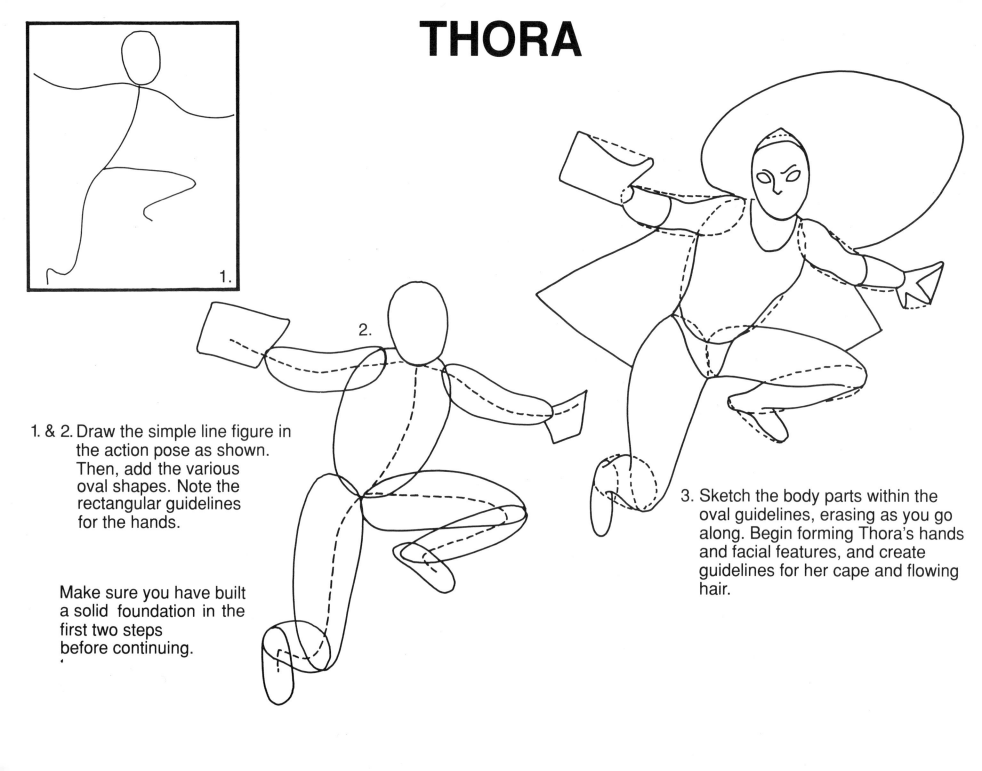

1. & 2. Draw the simple line figure in the action pose as shown. Then, add the various oval shapes. Note the rectangular guidelines for the hands.

Make sure you have built a solid foundation in the first two steps before continuing.

3. Sketch the body parts within the oval guidelines, erasing as you go along. Begin forming Thora's hands and facial features, and create guidelines for her cape and flowing hair.

5. Finish Thora's hair and cape, and add all the final details that will make this superheroine ready to spring into action.

4. Blend the body shapes together and complete the hands and face. Then, start forming her cape and long, flowing hair.

If you're not satisfied with the way any part of your drawing looks, erase it and start again.

CAPTAIN CRIMSON

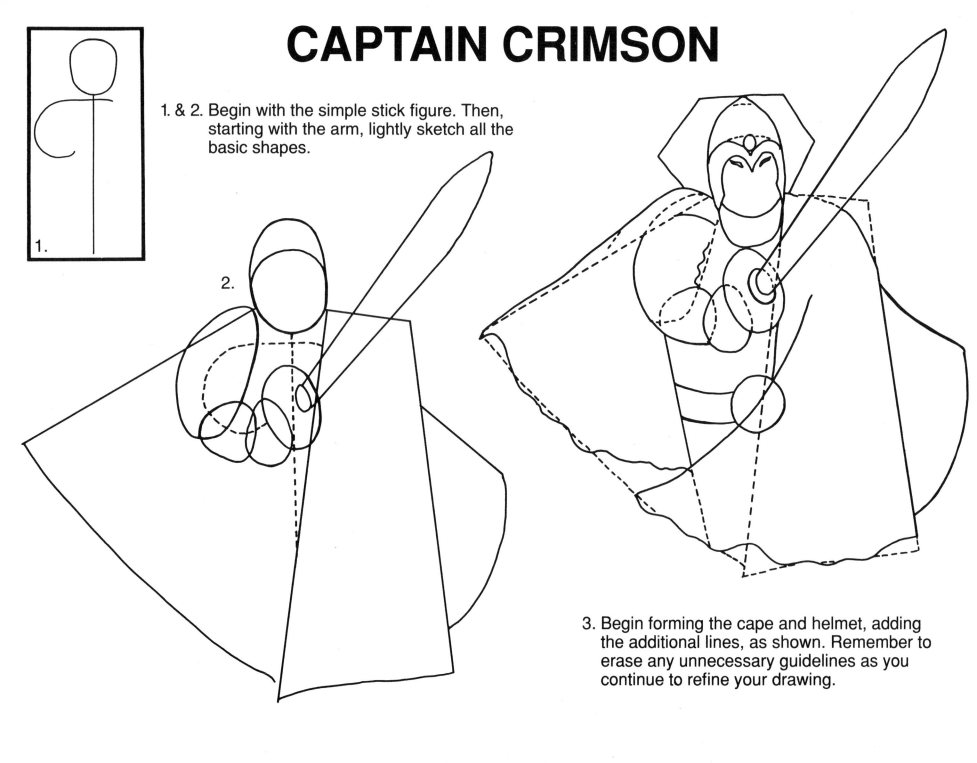

1. & 2. Begin with the simple stick figure. Then, starting with the arm, lightly sketch all the basic shapes.

3. Begin forming the cape and helmet, adding the additional lines, as shown. Remember to erase any unnecessary guidelines as you continue to refine your drawing.

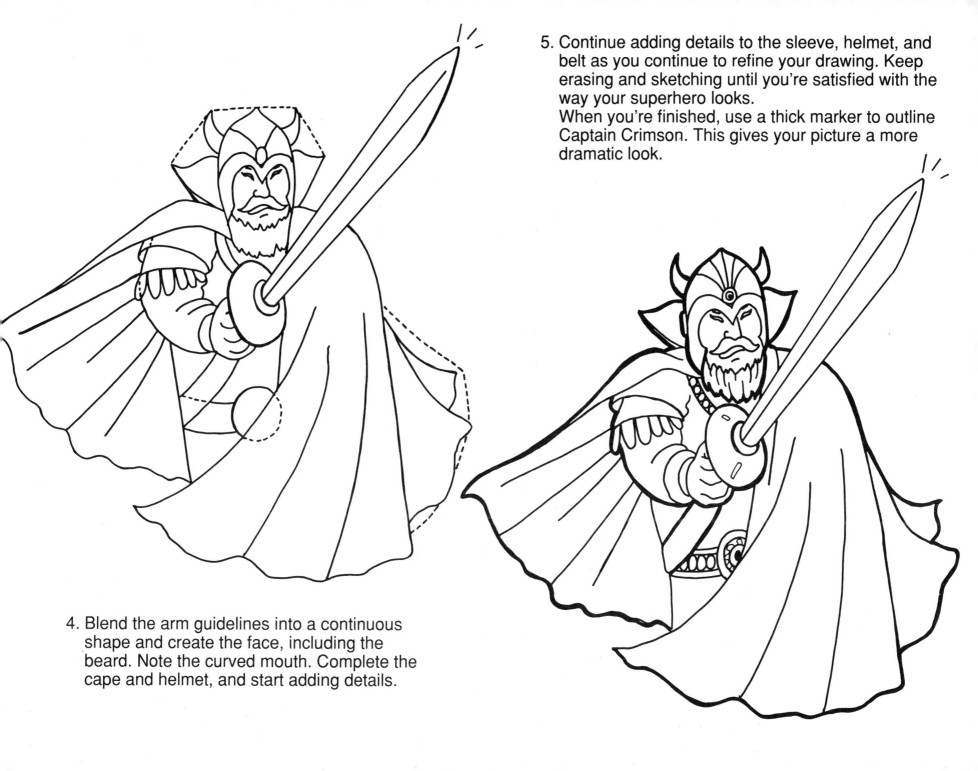

5. Continue adding details to the sleeve, helmet, and belt as you continue to refine your drawing. Keep erasing and sketching until you're satisfied with the way your superhero looks.
When you're finished, use a thick marker to outline Captain Crimson. This gives your picture a more dramatic look.

4. Blend the arm guidelines into a continuous shape and create the face, including the beard. Note the curved mouth. Complete the cape and helmet, and start adding details.

KARZAN
AND ZAP

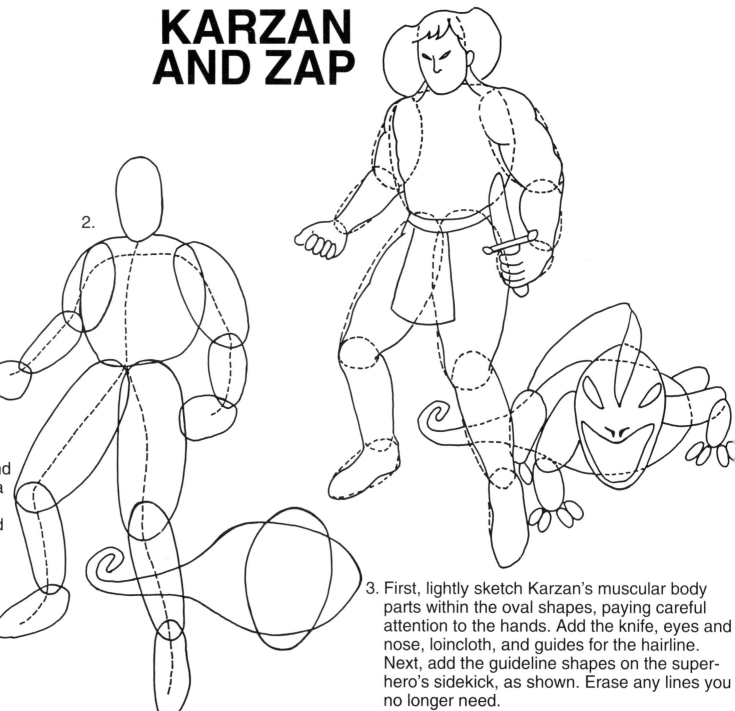

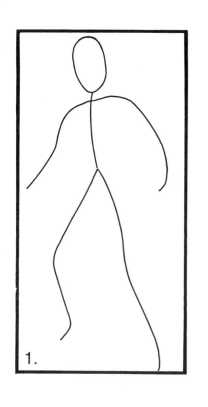

1.

2.

1. & 2. Lightly draw the stick figure and all the oval guideline shapes around it. This superhero has a friendly reptile, named Zap, for a sidekick. Add the two overlapping guideline shapes for the reptile.

3. First, lightly sketch Karzan's muscular body parts within the oval shapes, paying careful attention to the hands. Add the knife, eyes and nose, loincloth, and guides for the hairline. Next, add the guideline shapes on the super-hero's sidekick, as shown. Erase any lines you no longer need.

4. Blend the shapes into a smooth, muscular body. Add the boots, bow, arrow holder, facial features, and hair. Now start working on the smiling reptile. Create the wavy plate on Zap's back and the curved teeth and claws.

5. Add the remaining details, and Karzan and Zap are ready to face the unknown.

To draw scales:
Following the natural curves of the body, lightly draw the guideline rows, as shown. Then fill in each row with overlapping scales.

These are just a few of the weapons, masks,
shields, etc., that you can add to any of your superhero drawings.
Use your imagination and create many more.